Cross Stitching

Learn How to Cross Stitch
Quickly With Proven Techniques
and Simple Instruction

By Tatyana Williams

Table of Contents

Introduction

Cross stitch is a method of embroidery in which stitches are sewn in a tiled pattern to form letters or images. It is comparable to modern digital images created using pixels. The earliest American example of this work is from the 1600's, but there are likely European examples which are much older.

Cross stitch embroidery was often used to personalize and embellish useful household items such as napkins and dish cloths. However, it evolved into use for more decorative purposes, as well. It is now more frequently used to create images and sayings on pillow covers and wall hangings. Because of the way the thread is precariously anchored, it is generally not used on clothing.

There are several methods for threading the needle, for beginning the piece, for working the actual stitches and also for finishing the piece. There is not so much a right and wrong way so much as there are "ways that will look the best" and "ways which may be easier, but do not look as good."

The best way to start cross stitch is the old-fashioned way. Make your own pattern on a piece of graph paper, practice each style of stitching and create a "sampler" for reference. A sampler is a piece of cross stitch embroidery that was often made by young girls who were first learning the craft in order to practice their stitching while simultaneously creating a reference card for all the stitches they had learned. It was often decorative, as well, showcasing the alphabet, numbers 0-9, their name or perhaps a simple picture.

In this instructional booklet, we will learn everything from finding the middle of your fabric to creating your own patterns and using different stitches to change textures. Let's get started!

Chapter 1:
Glossary

Embroidery thread - The thread used to embroider or cross stitch. Also known as cotton/silk floss, stranded cotton/silk, or embroidery floss/silk. Embroidery thread also comes in silk, linen, wool, and rayon varieties.

Skein - The bundle of thread or floss that you buy, wrapped in a paper label containing the color number and the material from which the thread is made.

Strand – A single piece of embroidery thread.

Aida Cloth - The most frequently used fabric for cross stitching, woven into an even pattern so that each inch contains the same number of threads in both directions. There are holes between the threads for embroidery thread to pass.

Count/Stitch Count - The number of holes made by the threads in an inch of embroidery fabric.

Tail - The thread end that is left when beginning and ending a row of stitches.

(Full) Cross stitch – A simple embroidery stitch worked in an X (or cross) pattern.

Half Cross Stitch – A stitch made up of a single diagonal line of thread.

Quarter Cross Stitch – A diagonal stitch half the size of a half cross stitch.

Embroidery Frame/Hoop – A frame used for holding fabric in place while stitching. May be a circle, an oval or a rectangle with rollers (for larger pieces).

Embroidery Needles – A blunt tipped needle with an oversized eye for ease of use with larger threads.

Chapter 2:
Thread Basics

Embroidery thread comes in a a few different varieties. Typically, the kind you will want to use comes in small skeins of looped 6-stranded thread, bound by a paper wrapper. This is the most common type of thread.

There are other embroidery threads which come on larger spindles, but some of these have dyes which are not colorfast and may bleed dye onto the fabric if exposed to moisture. If you find a thread that you want to use, test its colorfastness by washing it with warm, soapy water, against a spare white rag to see if the color bleeds onto the white fabric.

The stranded skein should not be used at the full thickness in which it is sold. Instead, you will carefully pull out and cut a length of thread that is manageable. One end of the thread on the skein will pull the threads together and tangle, the other end will unravel freely from the rest. Use the second end to pull out the thread.

Cut the thread to the desired length. 18-24 inches will be good for most projects, but you will be doubling the thread, so pull out a length twice that amount. You don't want the doubled length of thread to be longer than your arm from shoulder to fingertip. If your project is quite small, use your arm as a guide for the full, un-doubled length.

Next, carefully separate the strands that are wound together and then gently remove a single strand of the thread from the others. Do this by holding the full thread and pinching the single strand*. It may help to push the other strands away from the single one you want to remove.

*Some projects will require thicker stitches, but for most projects, you will need only two strands, so double a single strand will be fine.

Once the skein has been unraveled, you can wrap strands around thread cards made of plastic or thick paper, for ease of use. Many kits that you buy will come with presorted threads that are already on a card of some kind.

Chapter 3:
Fabric

Cross stitch is typically done on a type of fabric known as "even-weave". The most commonly used type of even-weave fabric is known as Aida cloth.

Aida is made of cotton, but there are other types of even-weave – also sometimes called Java canvas – which are made of linen or other fabrics.

The edges of Aida cloth are delicate and, unless the type you purchase has been specially bonded or cut to keep it from fraying, may need to be sewed or taped down. If the piece is meant to be framed, regular masking tape will be fine. On the other hand, if the piece is meant for a pillow casing, then the edges should be sewn – by hand or on a machine – or it can be secured with special bias tape.

The count of the fabric determines how loose the weave is. Count is defined as holes per inch of Aida cloth. Larger count means a finer fabric that can hold more cross stitches, where it takes more stitches to make larger pictures. This type of fabric is usually reserved for tapestry-style work, or for smaller projects.

Fabrics come in a range of thread counts from very coarse (7) to very fine (22). The count size of the cloth you use will determine, in part, what size embroidery needle you use for your cross stitch project, as a larger needle will not fit through the smaller holes of a finer fabric.

The cloth comes in a variety of sizes and colors, and is even available on bolts like regular sewing fabric. Choose the color and size appropriate to the project you want to do – or buy a couple of yards off the bolt and cut pieces to fit your needs.

Chapter 4:
Needle Basics

The embroidery needles which are used for cross stitching are not sharp like regular hand sewing needles, but have rounded tips and extra long eyes for use with thicker thread and yarn. They are made for embroidering cross stitches in Aida cloth. These are also called crewel needles and are generally interchangeable with tapestry needles.

Size

The most commonly used sizes of crewel needle are the 24 and the 26. The larger the number, the smaller the needle size. Smaller needles should be used to embroider cross stitches onto cloth which has a higher thread count, as it will be harder for the larger needle to pass through the finer fabric without opening the hole too much.

Threading

You cannot tie knots on the back of cross stitch the way you do with regular hand sewing. The knots will show through the fabric. Therefore, you do not want to knot the thread when you thread your needle. Nor do you want to tie a knot in the tail to keep it from unraveling.

There are a few ways to thread the needle when preparing to cross stitch. How the needle is threaded determines, in part, how the piece will be finished on the back and how the tail is secured to keep the work from unraveling.

The easiest method – and one of the best looking finishes – is the **thread the needle using the cut ends**. Double the strand of thread you will be using for the first part of the project. Thread the cut ends of the thread into the eye of the needle, pulling them through only about an inch or two. This will leave a loop at the other end of your thread. When you make your first stitch, you will pass your needle inside that loop on the second pass, which will anchor the work in place and keep it secure.

Another method is to **thread the needle just as you would for regular sewing,** using the needle itself to create the loop that doubles the strand thickness. This method makes it much easier to keep from accidentally unthreading your needle while cross stitching, but will require special finishing to hide the beginning tail of the thread. You will work the first few stitches over the cut ends of the yarn to secure it in place.

A third method is to **thread the needle as for regular sewing adding a knot on the needle**. The knot on the needle will be cut before it reaches the fabric, so it will not be of issue. Once the thread is through the eye of the needle and doubled, then make a loop in the thread and pass the needle through it. This will make a knot in the yarn that will help keep the thread in place. It will be finished as in the previous method, but you will not have to keep adjusting your thread to make sure the double length remains even.

Chapter 5:
Patterns

A pattern or graph or chart is an image used for creating a cross stitch design on Aida cloth. It is made on graph paper and is coordinated with colors and/or symbols that tell you which type of stitch and color of thread to use where in a pattern. Most premade cross stitch kits will come with a pattern, as well as cloth and thread. Larger projects will divide the piece into multiple pages, whereas smaller pieces will be on a single page.

Reading

If the image is black and white, then the graph will usually use symbols to indicate which color thread to use for which portion of the image. When the graph is in color, symbols may be used to indicate what kind of stitch to use in different areas of the piece.

Sometimes, a lighter shading will indicate a different type of stitch than a cross stitch. A range of subtle texture effects can be achieved by using different kinds of stitching. This is something you will learn more about as you advance in your cross stitching skills.

Either way, there should always be a key on the graph, telling you what the symbols and shaded areas mean, such as ">=White (or the number of the thread color)" or "▉=half cross stitch."

There will also be arrows on most graphs to help you find the center of the image. It should correspond to the center of the fabric and this is where you should begin all your cross stitch work.

Creating

You can easily create your own patterns by using either graph paper or a spreadsheet program on your computer, such as Microsoft Excel or an advanced painting program such as Gimp. This is useful for beginners because you can create a practice pattern for yourself, to help you get the hang of the various stitches, before you attempt working a real pattern.

It is also useful for more advanced cross stitchers because you can make any image you want, without having to try to find a pattern that matches what you want to create. This is especially helpful when you want to create a personalized piece, like putting a name or a saying onto a pillow.

To create your pattern on graph paper, first write or draw the image or saying you wish to create with a dark pencil. Then fill in the appropriate squares so that each portion of the image is made up of cross or half or quarter stitches.

Excel is best for geometric patterns and names, though you can also use it to make simple images. You will fill in the appropriate boxes using the fill highlighter tool. You can select a range of colors and you can set the size of the boxes to fit your needs. When you are done, print it out – making sure the edges of the boxes are set to print - and you have your pattern.

With the pain program, there should be an option under the "View" menu to "show grid." There will be another place to set the default size for the grid. You will also want to "snap to grid" and use a paintbrush with a pixel size that corresponds to the size of a grid square. You can also start with an existing image this way and reduce it down so that it becomes pixilated and then blow it back up. Make sure the grid is set to print out with the image and print out your pattern.

Chapter 6:
Cross Stitch

The cross stitch itself is simple. The cross stitch is nothing more, really, than an "X" made out of thread. You will insert the needle into a hole in the Aida fabric and create one diagonal line, then cross it with another diagonal line. What is less simple is the inability to tie knots in the thread to secure it to the cloth. Therefore, how you begin the stitching and end it is very important and makes cross stitching more complicated than simply making a series of X's.

Methods of Beginning

If you are creating a single stitch, you insert the needle from back to front, through hole 1, as shown. Bring the needle back down through hole 3, up through hole 2 and down again through hole 4. *The red and blue line in the first image represents the tail that is on the back side of the yarn, which should be held so that it is caught up by the stitching on the back.*

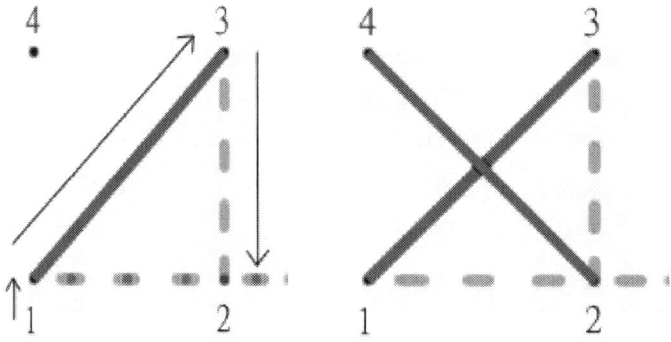

If you have threaded your needle so that the tail ends in a loop, you will pass the needle from back to front, leaving the loop sticking out in the back. Make the diagonal as shown in the previous picture, but when you pass the needle to the back side once more, come up through the loop of the tail, as shown, then back down into the next hole. This will secure the tail and keep the work from unraveling.

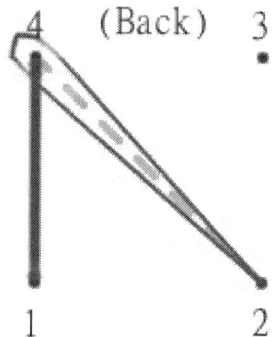

If you are making a row of stitches, it is better – and wastes less thread – to complete a row of half cross stitches and then come back and complete the row in the other direction. To do that, you start as if you were creating a single cross stitch, but then you take the needle across diagonally in the other direction.

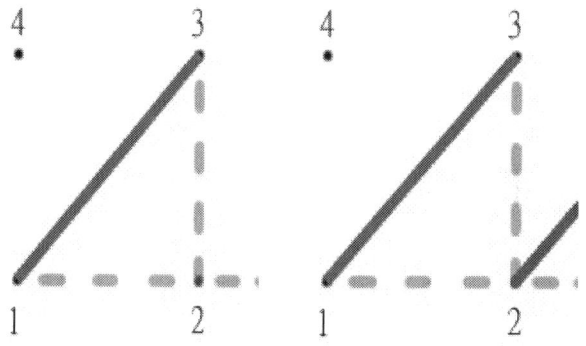

When you get to the end of the row, you repeat the process in reverse, making diagonal lines from the bottom right to the top left. If you are starting with a stack of cross stitch rows, it is better to start at the bottom and work your way up.

How to Finish

When you have reached the end of all the rows you are working in that color and section, or when your thread has gotten too short to continue (2"), complete the stitch you're working, ending with the needle in back. Slide your needle under the previous several stitches you've just worked – about 1-1.5" worth - and cut the thread level with the work. If desired, you may add a small dab of fabric glue to hold it in place, but avoid getting the glue on the Aida cloth.

Alternatively, you can finish by hiding both the beginning and ending tails on the *front* side of the work. This is really only for pieces where you are using more than two strands of thread and where the work will be framed and is in no danger of coming loose. To do this, you will start on the front, push your needle down through hole 4 and back up through hole 1. The tail will be held to the right as you work a row of half cross stitches over it.

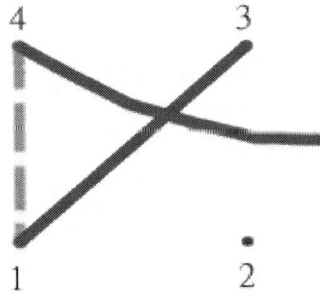

When you finish the row and have the end tail, you will finish as detailed in the first example, except you will complete the last stitch on the *front* of the cloth and slide the needle under front stitches before cutting the thread. This can be done even if you start with a looped beginning tail.

The benefit to this way of cross stitching is that it is actually a bit faster to work because you are always just sliding your needle from the top hole to the bottom one and can pinch the fabric to stitch through both holes with one movement.

Chapter 7:
Common Stitches

There are only a few basic stitches that are used in cross stitch patterns. The **Full Cross Stitch** is of course the primary stitch and is the familiar X pattern that covers one full square on Aida cloth. While it makes up the bulk of most stitching on a cross stitch project, there are a few types of smaller stitches, which are used to create texture, shaping, and shading on the piece.

Half Cross Stitch refers to a stitch which is just a single diagonal, without the cross. It is, in other words, half a cross stitch. This is used to create a subtle blurring effect on backgrounds and also to make a lighter shade without changing thread colors.

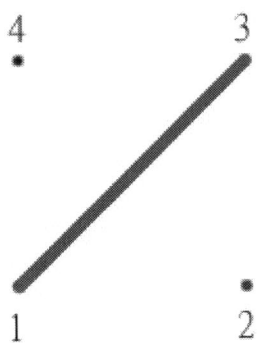

Quarter Cross Stitches are half of a half cross stitch. In other words, a quarter cross stitch is a single diagonal stitch, but it only extends half as far as a regular half stitch. This means that on Aida cloth, the needle will go through the fabric itself, rather than into one of the holes. On other weaves, full crosses go across three holes and the quarter stitch will go between two. This is used to create finer details.

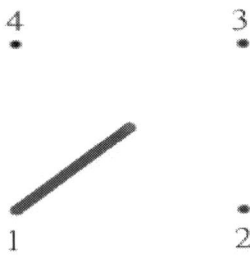

Three-Quarter Cross Stitches are a

combination of a half cross and a quarter cross, which go in opposite directions.

Back Stitching is used to outline the colored stitches to make them stand out and is generally done in black thread, often using fewer strands than the rest of the piece. It is done by bringing the needle up through the fabric as if you were going to cross stitch. You then bring your needle back down through the fabric - either diagonally, vertically or horizontally, depending on the shape you are outlining – but in the direction of the tail, not away from it. Each subsequent stitch is made by coming up in the next hole and coming down the hole you came out of on the previous stitch.

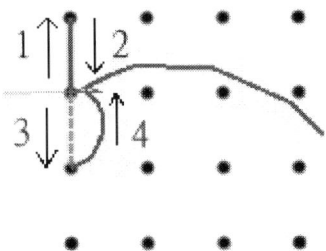

Chapter 8:
Tips and Tricks

It is important to have good lighting, a good pair of scissors and quality materials when learning to cross stitch. You should also make sure your hands are clean so that you don't get smudges on the cloth.

When using an embroidery hoop, only leave it on the piece while you are working. Take it off whenever you finish, so that it doesn't leave creases in your work. When using a rolling frame, make sure the work rolls under, so that the threads do not get worn and damaged.

Use a highlighter on larger patterns to keep track of what you've done. Every time you finish a section, highlight it so you will know it is done.

One easy way to thread your needle is to make a loop in the end of the thread by folding it around the needle and then stick the bent end into the eye and pull it through. This is easier (and less messy) than the "wet it with your mouth" method.

If your pattern calls for three quarter cross stitches around the edges, but you intend to outline the work in backstitch, make those edge stitches quarter cross stitches instead of three quarter. The outline will take care of the long diagonal.

Make a sampler for yourself like they did in days gone by. It will not only help you practice, but it will give you an easy reference for stitches and tricks when you've not embroidered for a while. It's also a nice keepsake that can be passed down.

If you want the cross stitch embroidery to look its best, make sure all your crosses are made with the same diagonal on top. If you find that you are crossing backward from the previous row, slide the needle under the existing diagonal before putting it back through the hole. This will make all the squares cross the same way.

You can increase the size of a pattern by counting each square as four stitches instead of one. In other words, a 2"x2" pattern would become 8"x8". You can decrease patterns by counting every four stitches as a single stitch.

Unfinished even-weave edges can be sewn by hand or on a machine. They can also be taped with masking tape, painter's tape or sewn down with bias tape.

Keep unfinished pieces that are not on roller frames in a bag or pillow case to protect the thread from snagging or getting dirty or dusty.

Chapter 9:
Basic Cross Stitch Patter 1

Materials - 1 skein of pink embroidery thread, 1 skein of black embroidery thread, 1 piece of Aida or other even-weave cloth at least 4"x4" square.

Tools - 1 crewel needle sized appropriately for the cloth count, small pair of scissors, highlighter (optional), masking tape (if needed)

Each pink "X" on the grid above represents one full cross stitch. Beginning in the middle, work full cross stitches (in a double strand of pink thread) into the cloth wherever X's are shown on the graph. Work quarter cross stitches wherever there is only a pink "/" or "\" symbol.

Finish by hiding tail in last stitches and trimming off. Use the black thread to backstitch wherever black "/", "\", "_"or "|" symbols appear.

Chapter 10:
Basic Cross Stitch Pattern 2

Materials - 2 skeins embroidery thread, in 2 different colors, one dark and one bright; 1 piece of Aida or other even-weave cloth at least 16"w x 14"h.

(Optional) 1 skein black and one skein in a pale color, for backstitching and background.

Tools - 1 crewel needle sized appropriately for the cloth count, small pair of scissors, highlighter (optional), masking tape (if needed)

	A	B	C	D	E	F	G	H	I	J	K	L	M	N	O	P	Q	R	S	T	U	V	W	X	Y	Z	AA	AB	AC	AD	AE	AF	AG	AH
1																																		
2																																		
3																																		
4						X		X		X	X	X	X		X			X		X	X	X	X											
5						X		X		X			X		X			X		X														
6						X		X		X			X		X	X		X	X		X								=	Color 1				
7						X	X	X	X	X			X		X		X		X	X	X	X	X						=	Color 2				
8						X		X		X			X		X			X		X														
9						X		X		X	X		X		X			X		X									=	Center				
10						X		X		X	X	X	X		X			X		X	X	X	X											
11																																		
12		O	O	O	O		O			O		O	O	O	O		O	O	O	O		O	O	O	O	O								
13		O			O			O		O							O								O									
14		O			O			O		O							O								O									
15		O	O	O	O		O			O		O	O	O	O		O	O	O	O		O			O									
16								O	O		O		O	O			O								O									
17								O	O	O		O	O		O		O								O									
18		O	O	O	O		O			O		O	O	O	O		O	O	O	O		O			O									
19																																		
20						X		X		X	X	X	X		X			X		X	X	X	X											
21						X		X		X			X		X			X		X														
22						X		X		X			X		X	X		X	X		X													
23						X	X	X	X	X			X		X		X		X	X	X	X	X											
24						X		X		X			X		X			X		X														
25						X		X		X			X		X			X		X														
26						X		X		X	X	X	X		X			X		X	X	X	X											
27																																		
28																																		
29																																		

Legend:
X = Color 1
O = Color 2
▨ = Center

Starting at the marked center, work full cross stitches in the bright colored thread over every spot marked by an "O" symbol.

Change to the darker color of thread and work a full cross stitch into every square with an "X" symbol.

Optional

Outline all cross stitches in black thread, using the backstitch.

Work a half cross stitch in the pale thread into all the white spaces directly next to any "X" or "O" space, to create a soft background color

Conclusion

If you follow the written instructions in conjunction with the pictures in this book, with practice and repetition you will be able to learn how to cross stitch in a very short period of time. If you are having trouble, just keep at it. Remember that error is a part of the process and patience is your friend.

Try all the different techniques listed for threading your needle and beginning a piece, so that you can find which ways work best for you and your embroidering style. Make your own patterns, buy kits or find patterns online and, above all *practice, practice, practice!* Today you may be make simple hearts and block letters, but soon you will be able to make complex pictures and patterns great for decorative gift giving.

Printed in Poland
by Amazon Fulfillment
Poland Sp. z o.o., Wrocław